A Practical Guide to

UTAH'S WILD EDIBLE PLANTS

A Practical Guide to
UTAH'S WILD EDIBLE PLANTS

STEVEN C. GOLIEB
PHOTOGRAPHS BY STEVEN C. GOLIEB

edible
wilds
EDIBLE WILDS LLC
PROVO

PUBLISHED BY
EDIBLE WILDS BOOKS
A SUBSIDIARY OF
LEO LASAGNA LLC
PROVO, UT

Library of Congress Cataloging-in-Publication Data

Golieb, Steven C. (Date__)
    A Practical Guide to Utah's Wild Edible Plants. --1st Edition
        p. cm.
    ISBN 0615905587

Back cover photography by: Lindsey Stallings Elem, www.lindseyelem.com

This book was made in conjunction with Edible Wilds, LLC of Eden, UT

www.ediblewilds.us

For my beautiful daughter Leitha.

CONTENTS

INTRODUCTION

Hello, and thank you for picking up this book! My name is Steven Golieb, and I am a specialist in edible and medicinal wild plants. I am the owner of Edible Wilds, LLC of Eden, UT, a company that produces food products from edible wild plants harvested locally in Utah. I give guided tours and seminars on how to survive in the wild eating exclusively from the native vegetation.

The need for this book became apparent after endless and unfruitful searches for information on wild vegetation specific to Utah. Currently, this is the only book in print that focuses entirely on Utah's wild medicinal and edible plants. All other books and guides available are aimed towards broad regions, such as the Rocky Mountain region, which spans over 3,000 miles over two countries and has a range of elevation of 14,440 feet high to as low as sea level. Clearly there are an overwhelming range of species and ecosystems that can inhabit that vast and diverse expansion of land. When focusing locally, however, the guides become almost entirely irrelevant; they become difficult to apply to specific areas (such as states) and contain a surplus of information that's hard to sift through. I felt the need to create a *practical* guide—one that could actually be of use to the Utah wilderness exclusively.

This book includes pictures, descriptions, and practical information on how to prepare and consume the different species available to the area. With each species represented in this book, a useful key is provided (left).

As you can see from the key sample (left), each species is star-rated on its abundance (how easy it is to find and how common a species it is to the area). The key also provides the seasons the species is available for harvest, its scientific information, as well as nutritional info. This feature makes finding a wild meal efficient, easy, and exciting!

Abundance: ★★★★
Seasons: **Spring**
Common Name: **Thistle**
Scientific Name: **Cirsium**
Family: **Asteraceae**
Nutrition:

-Fiber
-Ascorbic Acid*
-Chlorogenic Acid*
-Potassium*
-Inulin*
-Protein
-Calcium
-Cinarina*

* = Very high amounts

Many of the plants local to Utah have great medicinal purposes and properties. The medicinal uses are represented in the "Wild Medicine" section of the book.

There are many great benefits to learning about native plants and trees. Whether for survival, for fun, or for natural healing purposes, a great feeling of comfort and confidence can come from knowing ones surroundings while in nature. I sincerely hope this book can assist in better understanding nature, and hopefully that understanding can lead to a passion and furthered curiosity. Enjoy, and safe eating!

A WARNING

Before voyaging out in your neighborhood or in the wild in search for food, please take into consideration a few safety tips to ensure a successful and healthy harvest.

1) WEED KILLERS AND PESTICIDES-- Make sure to check for signs of spraying. If you are in an urban area, it is common for lawns and fields to be sprayed by chemicals. Make sure you are careful in what you harvest. Common signs of spraying is patches of dead weeds, browning of the leaves, and an abnormal change in height and health of the plant. It's also always a good policy to wash all harvested goods in water.

2) POISONOUS VARIETIES-- Most of the plants in this book have no "look-a-likes", or plants that are poisonous that resemble the edible ones. However, always take precautions. If you aren't sure what you're eating and you feel there's a chance it could be a different plant than the one in the book, just leave it alone. It's not worth risking it.

3) GENERAL RULE OF THUMB-- Though there are exceptions, and unless characterized in the description of the plant/tree in this book, the following are typical characteristics of poisonous plants and should be avoided:
   1. Milky or discolored sap
   2. Spines, fine hairs, or thorns
   3. Beans, bulbs, or seeds inside pods
   4. Bitter or soapy taste
   5. Dill or parsnip looking leaves
   6. "Almond" scent in the woody parts and leaves
   7. Grain heads with pink, purplish, or black spurs
   8. Three-leaved growth pattern

4) BUGS-- Many of the species mentioned in this book are frequented by a variety of insects. Make sure to wash all harvested goods thoroughly, and double check to make sure you've removed all insects. Many bugs can be poisonous or can cause severe sickness.

All in all, harvesting and consuming edible wilds plants is a very safe and fun activity. Just make sure you're taking precautions and you'll be just fine. Enjoy!

WILD EDIBLE PLANTS

Amaranth

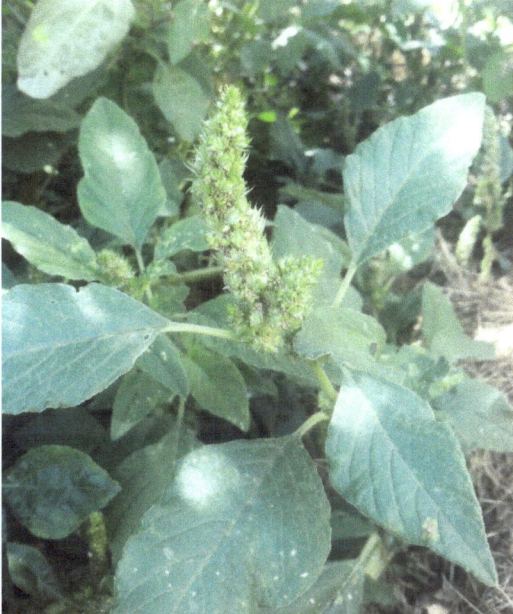

Abundance: ⭐⭐⭐
Seasons: **Spring, Summer**
Common Name: **Amaranth**
Scientific Name: **Amaranthus**
Family: **Amaranthaceae**
Nutrition:

-Vitamin E*
-Flavanoids*
-Calcium*
-Mangesium*
-Fatty acids*
-Vitamin A*
-Vitamin C*
-Manganese
-Magnesium

* = Very high amounts

Native to the Americas, all parts of the Amaranth plant are edible. The leaves of the plant contain oxalic acid. Although the acid is not poisonous and you may eat the plant raw, it is recommended to boil leaves in water to remove the acid. Do not use left over water. Amaranth can be found in well shaded or watered areas. They are very common weeds in gardens and lawns.

Roots: **N/A**
Leaves: **Edible**
Seeds: **Edible**
Stalks: E**dible**
Flowers/Buds: **Edible**

Practical Applications:
1) All parts of the plant can be eaten raw, though the leaves should be eaten in moderation due to presence of oxalic acid. If boiled, all parts of the plant can be eaten regularly.

Burdock

Abundance: ⭐⭐⭐
Seasons: **Spring, Summer**
Common Name: **Burdock**
Scientific Name: **Arctium**
Family: **Asteraceae**
Nutrition:

-Fiber*
-Phytosterols*
-Essential Fatty Acids*
-Calcium*
-Amino Acids*
-Potassium*
-Iron
-Protein
-Maganese

* = Very high amounts

Burdock is a relative of artichoke and has been used as a medicinal plant for thousands of years. It has been used as a blood purifier and kidney and liver cleanser, and its oils have been used for scalp treatment. Burdock can be found in many fairly-watered fields, abandoned lawns, forests and riverbanks. In summer Burdock produces a pink-colored flower that turns into a brown bur. This plant is considered invasive by many because of its burs.

Roots: **Edible**
Leaves: **Edible, not recommended**
Seeds: **Edible, not recommended**
Stalk: **Edible**

Practical Applications:
1) Burdock root is the most practical part of plant to eat. Dig out roots deep (do not try to pull out of ground, as it will break the stalk). Wash off roots and boil in water. Great source of essential vitamins and minerals, and it actually tastes great! Resembles flavor of artichoke and cauliflower.
2) Flower stalks can be harvested in spring before they mature or flower. Peel stalks thoroughly and eat raw.

Cattail

Abundance: ⭐⭐⭐
Seasons: **Summer**
Common Name: **Corndog Grass**
Scientific Name: **Typha**
Family: **Typhaceae**
Nutrition:

-Iron
-Phosphorus
-Dietary Fiber*
-Vitamin K*
-Vitamin B6*
-Calcium*
-Magnesium*
-Potassium
-Maganese

* = Very high amounts
** The nutritional info is for leaf shoots only.

Cattail is a very common and multifaceted survival food. Every part of the plant is edible and it provides a filling and nutritious meal. Cattails can be found near lakes, streams, river, ponds, and stagnant water all throughout Utah's valleys.

Roots: **Edible**
Leaves: **Edible**
Flowers/Seeds/Pollen: **Edible**
Stalk: **Edible**

Practical Applications:
1) The inner white core of cattail roots can be eaten raw or cooked. It can also be made into syrup or fermented to make alcohol.
2) Young shoots can be eaten raw, but do not mistaken with the iris plant, which is poisonous.
3) When plant is in active pollination, pollen may be collected and used as flour. Green flower sprouts can be boiled and eaten as corn-on-the-cob. Seeds can be ground as a flour or used in soups or breads.

Clover

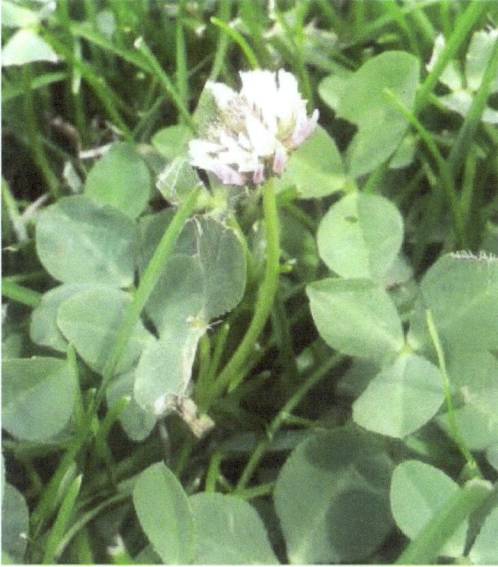

Abundance: ⭐⭐⭐
Seasons: **Spring, Summer**
Common Name: **Clover**
Scientific Name: **Trifolium**
Family: **Fabaceae**
Nutrition:

-Niacin*
-Chromium*
-Calcium*
-Mangesium*
-Phosphorus*
-Vitamin C*
-Potassium*
-Thiamine
-Magnesium*

* = Very high amounts

Clover is an incredible survival food often found in urban areas throughout Utah's valleys—mostly found in lawns or more watered areas. Originally introduced from Europe, three varieties of clover now grow throughout the United States, including Utah. The above picture is white clover, the most commonly-found clover in urban areas of Utah.

Roots: **Edible, not recommended**
Leaves: **Edible, best in spring**
Flowers: E**dible**
Seeds: **Edible**

Practical Applications:
1) Flowers can be eaten raw, fried or sauteed. They can also be used to make teas and wines or dried and ground into a flour. They can also be added to soups.
2) Leaves should be eaten in moderation unless cooked, as they are often difficult to digest. Leaves are best in springtime.
3) Roots are not recommended to eat, though they can be eaten after cooked.
4) Seeds can be ground into a flour or used medicinally.

Curly (Yellow) Dock

Abundance: ⭐⭐⭐⭐
Seasons: **ALL**
Common Name: **Curly Dock**
Scientific Name: **Rumex crispus**
Family: **Buckwheat/Smartweed**

Nutrition:

-Fiber*
-Vitamin A*
-Vitamin C*
-Calcium
-Phosphorus*
-Potassium
-Iron*
-Protein*
-Beta Carotene*
-Maganese

* = Very high amounts

Curly dock is one of the most commonly found edible wild plants in northern Utah. They can be found in fields, highway ditches, waste grounds, disturbed soils, riverbanks—virtually any abandoned or untouched area with lots of sun.

Roots: **Poisonous**
Leaves: **Edible, best in spring**
Seeds: **Edible, dried (reddish-brown colored)**
Stalk: **Interior edible**

Practical Applications:
1) Seeds are great to grind into a flour, soaked as oatmeal (add flavoring), or sprouted. Extremely high in Iron and Fiber. Similar flavor to buckwheat.
2) Leaves are best in spring and can be eaten raw as a salad in moderation. Leaves contain oxalic acid, which can be damaging to the body if consumed in high amounts. Best to boil leaves in several changes of water to remove oxalic acid.
3) Stalks can be peeled and boiled for a few minutes to soften. Great with salt.

Dandelion

Abundance: ⭐⭐⭐⭐⭐
Seasons: **Spring, Summer**
Common Name: **Common Dandelion**
Scientific Name: **Taraxacum O.**
Family: **Asteraceae**
Nutrition:

-Fiber*   -Vitamin E*
-Vitamin A*   -Vitamin K*
-Vitamin C*   -Thiamin
-Calcium   -Riboflavin*
-Phosphorus*   -Vitamin B6*
-Potassium
-Iron*
-Protein*
-Beta Carotene*
-Maganese

* = Very high amounts

Dandelion is by far one of the most nutritious and common plants found in Utah. Every plant of the dandelion is edible and is extremely beneficial. Be sure that you are harvesting dandelion safe from weed killers and/or other lawn chemicals.

Roots: **Edible**
Leaves: **Edible, best in spring**
Seeds: **Edible, not recommended**
Flowers: **Edible**
Stalk: E**dible**

Practical Applications:
  1) Leaves can be eaten raw and used as a salad. They are less bitter and most tender during springtime.
  2) Roots can be eaten raw, boiled, fried or dried and grounded. Roots can also create a wonderful medicinal tea.
  3) Flowers are edible and can be eaten raw. They can also make a great tea or can be used for coloring.

Grasses

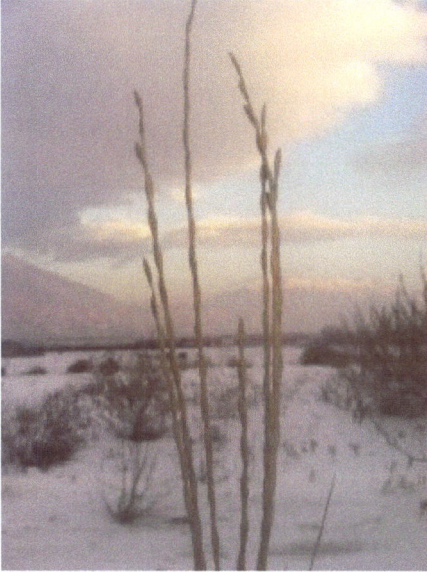

Abundance: ⭐⭐⭐⭐⭐
Seasons: **ALL**
Common Name: **Grasses**
Scientific Name: **Poaceae**
Family: **Poaceae**
Nutrition:

-Dietary Fiber*
-Manganese*
-Selenium*
-Iron*
-Niacin
-Thiamin
-Folate
-Phosphorus

* = Very high amounts

Grasses are one of oldest food sources for humans and animals alike. Found all throughout Utah's valleys, grasses are a wonderful survival food. Be sure to look for and avoid blackened grains as it can indicate an ergot infection. Ergot is a fungus that can cause serious illness and in some cases death.

Leaves: **Edible, best in spring**
Seeds: **Edible**
Stalk: E**dible**

Practical Applications:
1) Grains (seeds) are one of the most versatile parts of the grass plant. Grains can be ground to a flour, eaten raw or added to soups as a thickener.
2) The young shoots (leaves) of grasses can be eaten raw
3) The stalks of grasses can be eaten raw, boiled, roasted or pickled. They can even be dried and ground into a flour or meal.

Great Mullein

Photo Source: Wikipedia.org

Abundance: ⭐⭐⭐⭐
Seasons: **Spring, Summer**
Common Name: **Common Mullein**
Scientific Name: **Verbascum Thapsus**
Family: **Scrophulariaceae**
Nutrition:

Currently Unknown

* = Very high amounts

A very common plant of the western United States, the great mullein is mostly medicinal but the leaves can be made into a tea. The tea must be taken in moderation and is recommended to only be used medicinally. The seeds are toxic and should never be ingested.

Roots: **Not Edible**
Leaves: **Edible - Medicinal**
Seeds: **Poisonous**
Flowers: **Not Edible**
Stalk: **Not Edible**

Practical Applications:
1) Leaves can be boiled into a tea. However, tea MUST be strained multiple times to protect throat against tiny fibers on leaves as they can cause irritation.

Lamb's Quarters

Photo Source: Wikipedia.org

Abundance: ⭐⭐⭐⭐
Seasons: **Spring, Summer**
Common Name: **Pigweed**
Scientific Name: **Chenopodium Album**
Family: **Chenopodiaceae**

Nutrition:

-Niacin*
-Folate*
-Iron*
-Magnesium*
-Phosphorus*
-Dietary Fiber*
-Protein*
-Vitamin A*

-Riboflavin*
-Vitamin B6*
-Calcium*
-Potassium*
-Copper*
-Manganese*

* = Very high amounts

Extremely similar in taste and texture to spinach and closely related to Quinoa, lamb's quarters are extremely rich in nutrients and are a valuable survival plant. However, similar to curly dock and spinach, lamb's quarters is high in oxalic acid and should be eaten in moderation or boiled to remove the acid.

Roots: **N/A**
Leaves: **Edible, best in spring**
Seeds: **Edible**
Flowers: **Edible**
Stalk: E**dible**

Practical Applications:
   1) Lamb's quarters leaves and stalks can be eaten raw or boiled and have similar taste to spinach.
   2) Seeds can be eaten raw, grounded and can be used for sprouting. Lambs quarters seeds have been found in ancient archeological sites.
   3) Flower clusters can be eaten raw or can be added to soups.

Oregon Grapes

Photo Source: Wikipedia.org

Abundance: ★★★
Seasons: **Spring, Summer**
Common Name: **Pigweed**
Scientific Name: **Mahonia Aquifolium**
Family: **Berberidaceae**
Nutrition:

-Pectin*
-Vitamin A*
-Vitamin C*

* = Very high amounts

Oregon grapes can be found both in the more vegetated areas of the foothills but is also a common ornamental plant that can be found in urban areas. Though both edible and extremely medicinal, Oregon grapes should be avoided by pregnant women and should not be ingested when experiencing diarrhea. Berries should be eaten in moderation.

Roots: **Edible - Medicinal**
Leaves: **Edible - Young**
Flowers: **Edible**
Fruits: **Edible**
Stalk: **Not Edible**

Practical Applications:
1) Berries can be eaten raw, though they can be quite sour. They can be used to make jams, wine, or juices. The berries are full of antioxidants.
2) Very young and tender leaves can be eaten raw or boiled.
3) The roots are primarily medicinal and should only be really used as such, but they are edible if boiled.
4) The flowers are quite sour but can be added to foods for flavoring, such as salads or soups.

Plantain

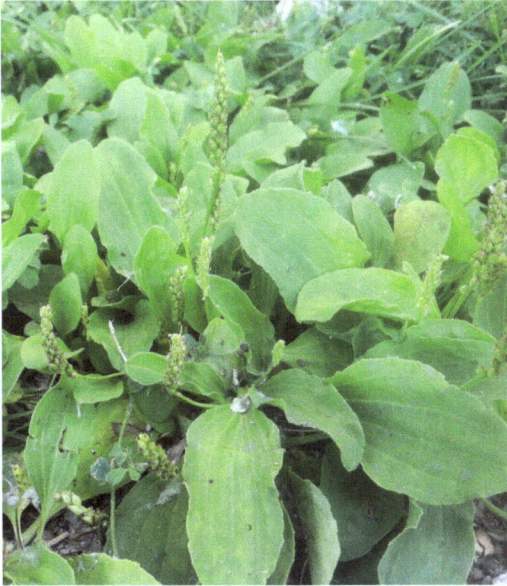

Abundance:
Seasons: **Spring**, **Summer**
Common Name: **Greater Plantain**
Scientific Name:
Plantago Major
Family: **Plantaginaceae**
Nutrition:

-Vitamin E*
-Vitamin K
-Calcium*
-Mangesium*
-Fiber*
-Vitamin A*
-Vitamin C*
-Manganese*
-Magnesium

* = Very high amounts

Plantains are quite abundant in the more rural or mountainous areas—they usually prefer well watered lawns or riverbanks. Tea made from its leaves can be used to treat diarrhea while replenishing the nutrients and minerals lost. It can be used as an anti-inflammatory, antioxidant, antibiotic, a boost to the immune system, and can be used to promote healing for wounds, sores and stings when leaves are applied. The sinews of mature plants can be used to make string as they are very pliable.

Roots: **N/A**
Leaves: **Edible**
Seeds: **Edible, but medicinal (see below)**
Stalks: **Edible, but not recommended**

Practical Applications:
1) Young leaves can be eaten raw. Older leaves are more tough and sour, so they can be boiled and eaten.
2) The seeds can be ground into a tea to treat sore throat and can promote bowel movements.
3) The leaves can be made into a tea, which can treat illness and replenish the body with important vitamins and minerals.

Purslane

Abundance: ⭐⭐⭐
Seasons: **Spring, Summer**
Common Name: **Pigweed**
Scientific Name:
Portulaca Oleracea
Family: **Portulacaceae**
Nutrition:

-Thiamin*
-Omega-3*
-Niacin*
-Vitamin B6*
-Folate*
-Vitamin A*
-Vitamin C*
-Riboflavin*
-Calcium
-Iron
-Magnesium
-Phosphorus
-Potassium
-Copper
-Manganese

* = Very high amounts

Purslane is a delicious and extremely nutritious plant found all throughout urban neighborhoods (in cracks in cement, weeds in garden beds, lawns, etc) and near bodies of water, such as streams and rivers. Purslane has more omega-3 fatty acids than any other leafy vegetable plant and is bursting with vitamins and minerals. It has a great taste and can be eaten as a salad or cooked in a variety of ways. Purslane has little yellow flowers and a soft foamy leaf.

Roots: **N/A**
Leaves: **Edible**
Flowers: **Edible**
Stalks: **Edible, but not recommended**

Practical Applications:
1) Purslane can be picked and eaten raw, boiled, steamed, fried and more. Can be added to soups and works great at a primary leafy green in salads.

Rabbitbrush

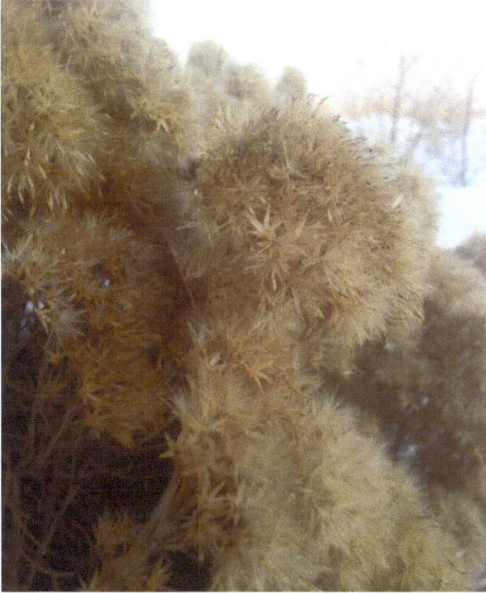

Abundance: ⭐⭐⭐⭐
Seasons: **Spring, Summer**
Common Name: **Rabbit Bush**
Scientific Name:
Chrysothamnus
Family: **Asteraceae**
Nutrition:

Currently Unknown

* = Very high amounts

Though mostly used as a medicinal plant, the Native Americans also used the sap and roots of the rabbitbrush as chewing gum. With yellow flowers present in the spring and summer times, rabbitbrush is a very common plant often found next to giant sagebrush.

Roots: **See Below**
Leaves: **Not Edible**
Seeds: **Not Edible**
Stalks: **Not Edible**

Practical Applications:
1) The bark of the roots can be peeled away, and when mixed with the sap, can be chewed as chewing gum.

Rose – Wild

Abundance: ⭐⭐
Seasons: **Spring, Fall**
Common Name: **Brier Hip**
Scientific Name: **Rosa Woodsii**
Family: **Rosaceae**
Nutrition:

-Vitamin E*
-Vitamin K
-Calcium*
-Mangesium*
-Fiber*
-Vitamin A*
-Vitamin C*
-Manganese*
-Magnesium
-Potassium

* = Very high amounts

Wild rose hips (the fruit of Roses) are one of Utah's wild delicacies. These wild roses flower from June to July and the pink pedals are edible if the white base of the pedal is removed quickly. The rose hip turns red when they ripen in late August through September. Rose hips are extremely nutritious—they contain approximately 60 times the amount of Vitamin C compared to lemons and 25 times more than oranges, ounce to ounce. Wild rose can be found in forested areas, but prefer mountainous riverbanks.

Roots: **Edible (see below)**
Leaves: **Not Edible**
Seeds: **Not Edible**
Fruit: **Edible**
Stalks: **Edible, but not recommended**

Practical Applications:
1) Rose hips are red in color when ripe. Can eat raw or boiled with seeds removed.
2) The roots, if rinsed and minced, can be made into a tea. Native Americans used the tea for cold symptoms and fevers.

Sagebrush

Photo Source: Wikipedia.org

Abundance: ⭐⭐⭐⭐⭐
Seasons: **Summer, Fall**
Common Name: **Sage**
Scientific Name: **Artemisia Tridentata**
Family: **Asteraceae**
Nutrition:

Currently Unknown

* = Very high amounts

Giant sagebrush, as opposed to the variety of sage used as a spice, is extremely high in volatile oils and is generally toxic to the liver and digestive system of humans. However, the seeds are edible and the plant offers many incredible medicinal benefits. Giant sagebrush is extremely common throughout Utah's valleys and foothills.

Roots: **Not Edible**
Leaves: **Not Edible**
Seeds: **Edible**
Stalks: **Not Edible**

Practical Applications:
1) Seeds can be collected in the late summer through fall and eaten raw or ground into meal, though the seeds are quit bitter.

Salsify

Photo Source: Wikipedia.org

Abundance: ⭐⭐⭐
Seasons: **Spring, Summer, Fall**
Common Name: **Salsifies**
Scientific Name: **Tragopogon**
Family: **Asteraceae**

Nutrition:

-Calcium
-Mangesium*
-Dietary Fiber*
-Vitamin B6*
-Vitamin C*
-Manganese*
-Magnesium*
-Thiamin
-Folate
-Pantothenic Acid
-Phosphorus
-Potassium*

* = Very high amounts

Salsifies are quite an incredible survival plant both medicinally and as food. With yellow or purple dandelion-like flowers, salsifies can be found throughout Utah's valleys. (The purple salsifies are called "common salsify" and the yellow "yellow salsify". The common salsify often has larger and tastier roots.

Roots: **Edible (see below)**
Leaves: **Edible - Young**
Seeds: **Edible - Sprouting**
Stalks: **Edible - Young**

Practical Applications:
  1) The big roots can be eaten raw, boiled roasted or fried before flower stalks appear.
  2) Young leaves and flower buds can be eaten raw.
  3) Young stalks can be steamed or simmered, much like asparagus.
  4) Seeds can be collected, stored and used for sprouting.

Smooth Sumac

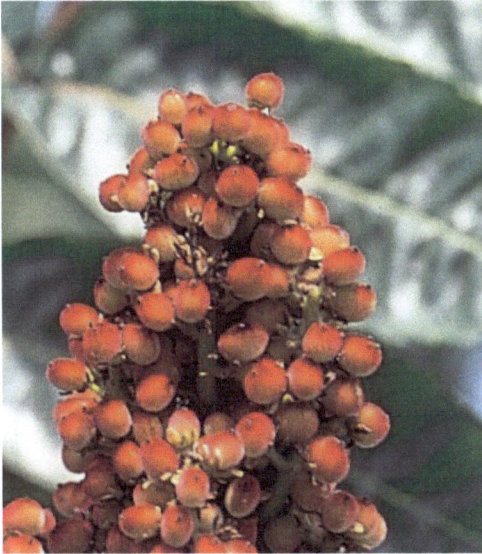

Photo Source: Wikipedia.org

Abundance: ⭐⭐⭐
Seasons: **Summer**
Common Name: **Sumac**
Scientific Name: **Rhus glabra**
Family: **Rosaceae**
Nutrition:

-Vitamin C*

* = Very high amounts

**There haven't been many studies on nutritional facts.

Smooth Sumac is a small to large shrub that lives primarily in the lower elevations of Utah. Commonly found near roadways, plains and foothills, or sometimes used as an ornamental shrub, sumac offers berries that taste much like lemons. They can be used to make a lemonade-like drink or can be eaten raw to relieve thirst.

Roots: **Not Edible**
Leaves: **Not Edible**
Seeds: **Not Edible**
Fruit: **Edible**
Stalks: **Not Edible**

Practical Applications:
  1) The fruits of the sumac can be eaten raw or used as flavoring. Best to remove hairs through straining with water or rubbing with cloth.

Sunflower

Abundance: ⭐⭐⭐⭐
Seasons: **Spring, Summer**
Common Name: **Sunflower**
Scientific Name:
Helianthus Annuus
Family: **Asteraceae**
Nutrition:

-Fiber
-Iron*
-Pantothenic Acid
-Vitamin B6*
-Niacin*
-Thiamin*
-Riboflavin*
-Omega Fatty Acids
-Phosphorus*
-Copper*
-Manganese*
-Magnesium*
-Potassium
-Protein*

* = Very high amounts

Sunflowers are extremely common along roadsides and vacant fields throughout the state of Utah. Most commonly found in sunny areas, sunflowers are very nutritious and all parts of the plant (aside from its tiny roots) are edible.

Roots: **N/A**
Leaves: **Edible**
Seeds: **Edible**
Stalk: **Edible**

Practical Applications:
1) Most obviously, sunflower seeds are edible, though most wild varieties have very small seeds. Can be eaten raw or roasted.
2) The stalks of sunflower plant can be boiled until soft and eaten plain.
3) The young flower buds in early to late spring can be eaten boiled until soft, similar to artichoke hearts.
4) Eating the leaves of a sunflower is not a wonderful experience, but if desperate, can be eaten boiled.

Thistle

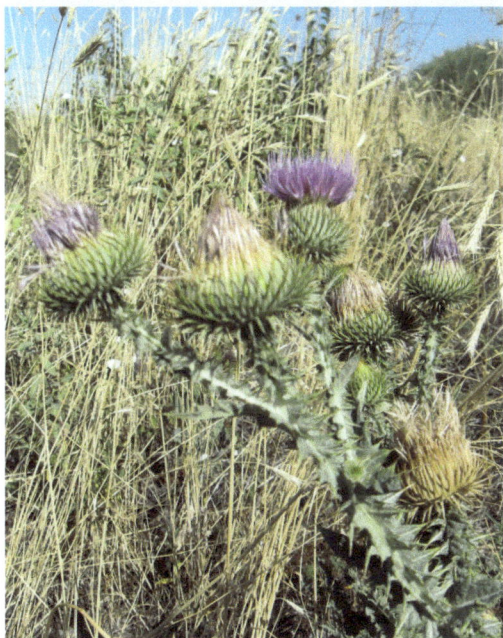

Abundance: ⭐⭐⭐⭐⭐
Seasons: **Spring**
Common Name: **Thistle**
Scientific Name: **Cirsium**
Family: **Asteraceae**
Nutrition:

-Fiber
-Ascorbic Acid*
-Chlorogenic Acid*
-Potassium*
-Inulin*
-Protein
-Calcium
-Cinarina*

* = Very high amounts

One of the most commonly-found weeds in Utah are Thistles. Though they are pests to many, they are also edible and may be a great source of food when in a survival situation. Thistles can be found virtually in any sunny climate in Utah, and are mostly only edible during spring (or when plant is green). Be sure to use gloves while handling them!

Roots: **N/A**
Leaves: **Edible**
Seeds: **Edible**
Stalk: **Edible**
Flower Buds: **Edible**

Practical Applications:
1) Use sharp knife to strip away outer skin from stalks. Inner stalks can be eaten raw, boiled or steamed.
2) Flower buds (before matured) can be boiled. Peel flower bud after boiling. Soft inner core is edible.
3) Leaves can be eaten boiled. Cut off thorns then boil.
4) Seeds are edible. Can be eaten boiled, or if you have a machine to produce oil, 12 pounds of seeds will produce 3 pounds of oil.

WILD EDIBLE TREES

Aspen

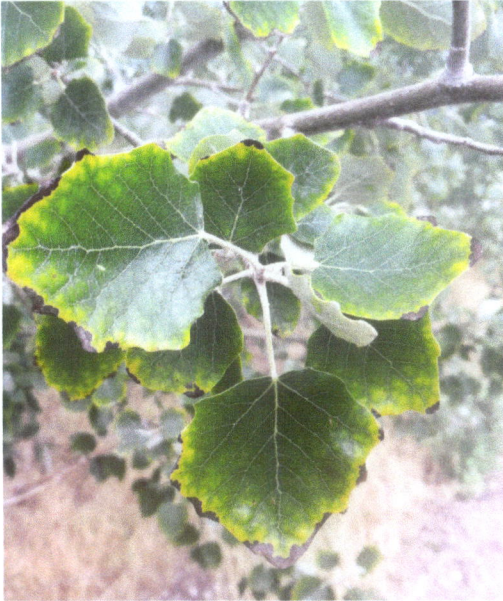

Abundance: ⭐⭐⭐⭐
Seasons: **Spring, Summer**
Common Name: **Aspen**
Scientific Name: **Populus Tremuloides**
Family: **Salicaceae**
Nutrition:

-Vitamin C*

* = Very high amounts

Aspens are very common in Utah. They are both used as an ornamental tree throughout urban neighborhoods as well as throughout higher elevations. Similar to Cottonwood trees, many Native American tribes stripped the tender inner bark in springtime and used them as a sweet treat for kids. The tree also has incredible medicinal properties, such as killing parasitic worms and treating fevers, inflammation, pain, diarrhea, jaundice, urinary tract infections and more.

Leaves: **Edible – See Below**
Bark: **Edible - Inner**
Flower Buds: **Edible – See Below**

Practical Applications:
1) Use a sharp knife to strip away rough outer bark to gain access to soft, tender inner bark in springtime. Can be eaten raw.
2) Young leaf buds and catkins can be eaten raw and are very high in Vitamin C, though bitter.

Blue Spruce

Abundance: ⭐⭐⭐⭐⭐
Seasons: **Spring**
Common Name: **Colorado Spruce**
Scientific Name: **Picea pungens**
Family: **Pinaceae**
Nutrition:

Currently Unknown

Blue Spruce is Utah's state tree and is one of the most commonly-found trees throughout the state. Both found in urban neighborhoods planted as an ornamental tree as well as throughout canyons and mountain-land, the Blue Spruce offers a wide range of support to the survivalist. All evergreens, however, should be eaten in moderation.

Roots: **Not Edible**
Leaves: **Edible - See Below**
Stalk: **Edible - See Below**
Bark: **Not Edible - Medicinal**

Practical Applications:
1) Young shoots can be eaten raw or cooked. Sources suggest not to eat the young needles with the shoots, but there has been no significant evidence showing any related health issues.
2) Inner bark can be accessed through cutting away rough outer bark. Dried inner bark can be ground into a nutritious flour.

Cottonwood

Abundance: ★★★★
Seasons: **Spring**
Common Name: **Balsam Poplar**
Scientific Name: **Populus Balsamifera**
Family: **Salicaceae**
Nutrition:

Currently Unknown

Cottonwood trees are one of the most despised trees throughout the warmer months of the year by many due to its allergenic properties, but the tree also has a sweet side. Many Native American tribes used the inner bark of the tree as a sweet treat for kids in the springtime while the sap was flowing. Cottonwoods can be found throughout the valleys both in urban neighborhoods or anywhere near water.

Roots: **N/A**
Leaves: **Edible**
Seeds: **Edible**
Stalk: **Edible**
Flower Buds: **Edible**

Practical Applications:
1) Use a sharp knife to cut off the rough outer bark to get access to the tender, sweet and translucent inner bark in spring time. Can be eaten raw in large quantities.
2) Young catkins can be eaten, though they may sometimes irritate skin.

Juniper

Abundance: ⭐⭐⭐
Seasons: **ALL**
Common Name: **Juniper**
Scientific Name: **Juniperus**
Family: **Cupressaceae**
Nutrition:

-Copper
-Chromium
-Calcium
-Iron
-Limonene
-Phosphorous
-Magnesium
-Potassium
-Vitamin C

* = Very high amounts

One of the most commonly-found trees in Utah, Juniper provides incredible medicinal properties and offers a consistent source of food. There are many varieties of Juniper, though the most common variety found in Utah is the "Rocky Mountain Juniper." Although the berries are edible, it is not recommended to eat large amounts or for an extended period of time due to their strong medicinal properties. People with liver problems nor pregnant women should ingest any part of the Juniper.

Roots: **Not Edible**
Leaves: **Not Edible - Medicinal**
Fruit: **Edible - In Moderation**
Branches: **Not Edible**

Practical Applications:
1) Juniper berries are available all year round, though the sweetest berries have been through at least two seasons. Juniper berries have a very strong piney taste and are often better eaten dried or roasted.
2) Branches and leaves can be boiled into a tea, though it is extremely high in medicinal properties and can be toxic in high doses.

Maple

Abundance: ⭐⭐⭐
Seasons: **Spring**
Common Name: **Thistle**
Scientific Name: **Acer**
Family: **Sapindaceae**
Nutrition:

-Potassium
-Calcium
-Magnesium
-Manganese
-Iron
-Zinc

* = Very high amounts

Maple is best known for it's syrup which is available in early spring time, when the tree wakes up and starts distributing its sap throughout its trunk. There are three commonly-found maples found throughout Utah: Box Elder, Rocky Mountain Maple and Norway maple. Box Elder is typically found in higher elevations near riverbeds or canyons, Rocky Mountain Maple grows in moist rocky mountainous areas, and Norway Maple is a common ornamental tree that can be found in urban neighborhoods. This tree can provide wonderful watery sap filled with probiotics and nutrients.

Leaves and Roots: **Not Edible**
Seeds: **Edible - Not Recommended**
Sap: **Edible**

Practical Applications:
1) Sap can be extracted from the tree in early-mid spring by carving a small but deep hole in the tree. You can carve a small wooden wedge to fit in the hole as a tap. Sap can be drank raw (similar to water infused with minerals) or it can be boiled down to a syrup.
2) Some varieties of maple produce edible seeds, but it's best to avoid as it is difficult to decipher.

Oak

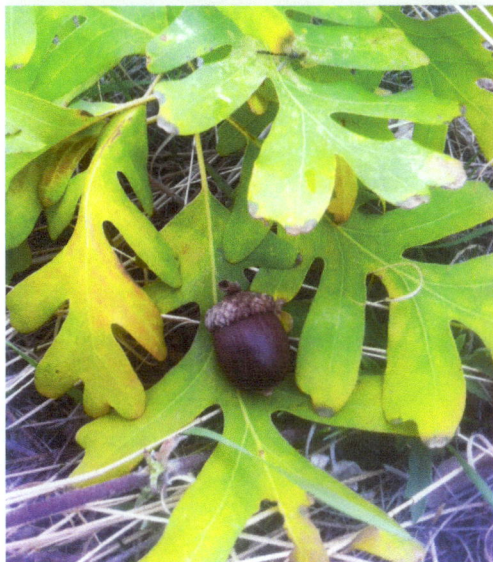

Abundance: ⭐⭐⭐
Seasons: **Summer, Fall**
Common Name: **Gambel Oak**
Scientific Name: **Quercus Gambelii**
Family: **Fagaceae**
Nutrition:

```
-Fiber
-Protein*
-Vitamin B6*
-Manganese
-Copper
-Potassium
-Calcium
-Folate

* = Very high amounts
```

The most commonly-found oak tree in Utah is the gambel oak, which has the sweetest acorns of all other varieties, though they are still quite bitter. Gambel oak often appears quite shrub-like and can be found on the mid to lower sides of the mountains. The acorns were a major staple food for many Native Americans.

Roots: **Medicinal - Inner**
Leaves: **Not Edible**
Seeds: **Edible**
Bark: **Medicinal - Inner**

Practical Applications:
1) Acorns can be eaten raw, although they are quite bitter due to high levels of tannin. If eaten raw, remove outer shell before eating inner nut.
2) To remove bitterness, acorns can be roasted while in shell by placing them on stones placed over hot coals. An additional option for removing bitterness is by soaking the raw nuts (with shells removed) in multiple batches of water. This process can take 1-3 weeks.
3) Ground nuts can be used as a thickener for soups or baked into muffins, breads or pancakes.

Russian Olive

Abundance: ⭐⭐⭐⭐⭐
Seasons: **Summer**
Common Name: **Silver Berry**
Scientific Name:
Elaeagnus Angustifolia
Family: **Elaeagnaceae**
Nutrition:

-Vitamin E*
-Flavanoids*
-Calcium*
-Mangesium*
-Fatty acids*
-Vitamin A*
-Vitamin C*
-Manganese
-Magnesium

* = Very high amounts

Russian Olive trees are one of the most commonly found wild trees in Utah. Though they are considered an invasive species, they are a good source of food in mid to late summer. The fruit is dry, sweet and mealy. It can be eaten raw. The seeds of the fruit is also edible, but is quite fibrous and may be better eaten cooked. You can find the Russian Olive tree in virtually any type of soil in the lower elevation areas, such as valleys. They look like giant sage brush trees and have yellow flowers in the spring. The fruit are ripe in mid to late summer.

Roots: **Not edible**
Leaves: **Not edible**
Seeds: **Edible**
Stalks: **Not edible**
Fruit: **Edible**

Practical Applications:
1) Only the fruit of the tree is edible. Can be eaten raw or cooked. Dried fruit can be mixed with milk to treat joint pain and rheumatoid arthritis.

Willow

Abundance: ★★★★
Seasons: **Spring, Summer**
Common Name: **Sandbar Willow**
Scientific Name: **Salix Exigua**
Family: **Asteraceae**
Nutrition:

-Vitamin C*
-Salicin*

* = Very high amounts

While many varieties of willow are edible, they are mostly used medicinally. The most commonly-found variety in Utah is sandbar willow, which mostly grow by lakes, rivers and streams, though many have been planted as an ornamental tree. Sandbar willows are mostly shrub-like in appearance and have long slender leaves.

Roots: **N/A**
Leaves: **Edible – Young Shoots**
Bark: **Edible – Inner**
Stalk: **Edible – Young Shoots**
Flower Buds: **Edible – Young Buds**

Practical Applications:
1) The young shoots and leaves, inner bark and flower buds are edible. They can be eaten raw or cooked and are extremely high in Vitamin C.
2) Willow has many strong medicinal properties. As a warning, do not ingest tree in high dosages. People who are allergic or irritable to aspirin should not ingest willow.

WILD MEDICINE

Antibiotics & Antibacterials

Curly Dock:

    The seeds and leaves of dock plants have anti-bacterial properties due to its high levels of anthraquinones. It can also act as a mild laxative and combat ringworm's and other fungi.

Juniper:

    Juniper berries contain antibiotic compounds and can be eaten raw or made into a tea to combat tumors.

Oak:

    Tannic acid, which can be found in acorns, is an anti-bacterial and anti-viral.

Plantain:

    Ingesting the raw leaves of plantains have anti-bacterial properties due to containing high levels of flavonoids.

Animal / Insect Bites

Burdock:
Seeds of burdock can be used as a poultice to treat insect bites and snake bites.

Clover:
Clover plants can be boiled in water to create a tea that can be used as an antidote for many poisonous bites and stings by scorpions and snakes.

Maple Tree:
Tea made from the branches of maple trees can treat snake bites when applied both externally & internally.

Oak:
Tea made out of oak bark can be used to treat insect bites.

Plantain:
The juices of plantain leaves can be applied to the skin to treat snake bites, insect bites and stings.

Salsify:
Tea made from all of the edible parts of the plant have been used to treat bites from coyotes both internally and externally.

Spruce:
Spruce sap mixed with fat can be used to create a salve to treat insect bites.

Sunflower:
Sunflower leaves can be applied topically as a poultice to treat spider bites and snake bites.

Blood Sugar

Burdock:
    Burdock root has shown to reduce sugar levels in blood.

Dandelion:
    The roots of a dandelion can be eaten raw or boiled and ingested to lower blood sugar, lower blood pressure, and lower cholesterol levels.

Juniper:
    Juniper berries, when eaten raw, have been used to balance (lower) blood sugar levels that has been effected by adrenaline hyperglycemia.

Smooth Sumac:
    Tea created from the berries of the smooth sumac was used to treat diabetes.

Blood / Organ Issues

Burdock:
Ingestion of burdock root (boiled) has been shown to purify the blood, act as a liver tonic, treating liver, gout and kidney problems, high blood pressure, measles, vertigo, rheumatism and gonorrhea. Burdock root has also been used to dissolve bladder stones.

Clover:
Red clover (*trifolium pratense)* can be eaten raw or made into a tea to act as a blood purifier, a blood thinner, or it can be used to remove toxins from the blood.

Dandelion:
The roots of a dandelion can be eaten raw or boiled and ingested to lower blood sugar, lower blood pressure, and lower cholesterol levels. Tea made from the roots or leaves of dandelion can treat liver and urinary tract problems. Ingesting dandelion flowers can treat liver problems, such as jaundice.

Great Mullein:
Tea made from mullein leaves can treat kidney infections. However, tea MUST be strained multiple times to protect throat against tiny fibers on leaves as they can cause irritation. WARNING: seeds of the great mullein are poisonous.

Cold Symptoms

Clover:
Clover plants can be boiled in water to create a tea to be taken internally to treat cold symptoms such as fever, cough and sore throat.

Cottonwood:
The bark of cottonwood has been chewed to improve cold symptoms. Cottonwood bark can also be made into a tea for treating whooping cough and tuberculosis. Sticky resins from the flower buds can be collected in spring and ingested to treat coughs and pain.

Juniper:
Native Americans have created tea using juniper branches and cones to treat coughs, pneumonia, fevers and colds. Juniper berries can also be chewed to treat colds. Native Americans would also burn juniper branches and inhale the smoke to relieve chest infections and colds.

Rabbitbrush:
Rabbitbrush roots can be boiled into a tea to treat cold symptoms, coughs and fevers. Tea can also be made from the leaves to treat colds and reduce fever.

Sage:
Tea made from sage leaves can treat fevers, colds, coughs and pneumonia.

Smooth Sumac:
Sumac berry tea had been used to treat fevers.

Spruce:
Sap from spruce trees can be boiled in water and used to treat coughing and sore throat. Needles can be boiled and chewed to relieve coughing. Tea made from the inner bark can be inhaled to relieve bronchitis.

Sunflower:
The flowers of sunflowers can be made into a tea to treat high fevers and headaches.

Thistle:
The leaves of the thistle plant can be made into a medicinal tea to treat cold symptoms such as fevers and strengthen the stomach.

Willow:

      The bark of the willow tree can be made into a tea to treat fevers and headaches.

Cough / Throat

Cattail:
    Chewing the leaves and stalks of cattail can treat or relieve sore throat and coughing.

Clover:
    Clover plants can be boiled in water to create a tea to be taken internally to treat cold symptoms such as fever, cough and sore throat. The flowers of red clover can be made into a tea to treat asthma.

Cottonwood:
    Sticky resins from the flower buds can be collected in spring and ingested to treat coughs and pain. Cottonwood bark can also be made into a tea for treating whooping cough and tuberculosis.

Juniper:
    Native Americans would burn juniper branches and inhale the smoke to relieve chest infections. Native Americans also created a tea using juniper branches and cones to treat coughs and pneumonia.

Oak:
    Oak bark tea can be used to relieve sore throats.

Plantain:
    Plantain tea, made from seed stalks and leaves, have been used for hundreds of years as a treatment for coughs, laryngitis, bronchitis, tuberculosis, sore throat and mouth sores.

Rabbitbrush:
    Rabbitbrush roots can be boiled into a tea to treat cold symptoms, coughs and fevers.

Rose:
    Rose roots can be boiled into a tea that can be gargled to reduce swelling and treat sore throat and tonsillitis.

Sage:
    Tea made from sage leaves can treat headaches, fevers, colds, pneumonia and coughing.

Spruce:
    Sap from spruce trees can be boiled in water and used to treat coughing and sore throat. Needles can be boiled and

chewed to relieve coughing. Tea made from the inner bark can be inhaled to relieve bronchitis.

Sunflower:

The flowers of a sunflower can be made into a tea to treat lung problems. The oil from sunflower seeds can be used to treat coughs and laryngitis.

Smooth Sumac:

The roots of smooth sumac can be chewed to relieve sore throats. The branches of the tree can be made into a tea to treat tuberculosis.

Cuts & Wounds

Cottonwood:
Leaves can be applied to sores, boils, aching muscles and bruises that have been infected by maggots. Mixing flower buds (available in spring) with fat can be used as a salve that can treat skin infections and treat aching muscles.

Juniper:
Oils from juniper berries would often be used to protect wounds from flies by mixing them with fat to make salves.

Lambs Quarters:
The leaves of lambs quarters can be used as poultices to treat wounds, swelling and burns.

Sage:
Ground sage leaves can be applied to cuts to combat infection.

Salsify:
The white sap of salsify plants can be applied to open sores and wounds to stop bleeding and oozing.

Smooth Sumac:
The bark from the roots of smooth sumac can be used as a poultice to heal open wounds.

Spruce:
Sap from spruce trees can be mixed with fat to create a salve for treating cuts, rashes, scrapes and burns.

Willow:
Poultices made from the inner bark can be applied to insect bites, cuts, rashes, cancers, minor burns and scrapes.

Headache

Great Mullein:
Tea made from mullein stalks can treat migraine headaches. However, tea MUST be strained multiple times to protect throat against tiny fibers on leaves as they can cause irritation. WARNING: seeds of the great mullein are poisonous.

Lambs Quarters:
The bruised leaves of lambs quarters can be applied to the head when experiencing headaches.

Plantain:
Plantain roots can be boiled and eaten or made into a tea for treating headaches.

Rose:
Rose petals can be eaten to treat headaches.

Sage:
Tea made from sage leaves can treat headaches, fevers, colds, coughs and pneumonia.

Sunflower:
The flowers of a sunflower can be made into a tea to treat headaches.

Willow:
Willow bark can be chewed or made into a tea to treat headaches.

Infections & Parasites

Aspen:
   Tea made from aspen bark has been used to treat urinary tract infections and to kill parasitic worms.

Burdock:
   Burdock leaves can be made into a wash (tea) that can treat skin infections.

Cottonwood:
   Leaves can be applied to sores, boils, aching muscles and bruises that have been infected by maggots. Mixing flower buds (available in spring) with fat can be used as a salve that can treat skin infections and treat aching muscles.

Curly Dock:
   Ingesting the leaves and seeds of dock plants can combat ringworm's and other fungi due to its high levels of anthraquinones.

Great Mullein:
   Tea made from mullein leaves can treat kidney infections. However, tea MUST be strained multiple times to protect throat against tiny fibers on leaves as they can cause irritation. Flowers from mullein can be soaked in oil and applied topically to treat ear infections.

Plantain:
   Plantain seeds and seed stalks can be used to make a tea to treat intestinal worms due to containing high levels of mucilage.

Sage:
   Ground sage leaves can be applied to cuts to combat infection. Sage leaves can also be soaked in water and applied as a poultice to treat infection and swelling.

Spruce:
   Sap from spruce trees can be mixed with fat to create a salve for treating infections.

Thistle:
   The leaves of the thistle plant can be made into a medicinal tea to kill intestinal worms.

Smooth Sumac:

Tea made from smooth sumac berries has been used to treat ringworm.

Pain & Inflammation

Aspen:
    Due to its high levels of salicin, young leaves from the aspen tree can be ingested to relieve fevers, pain and inflammation.

Cattail:
    Root-stocks can be made into a paste to treat inflammation. The root-stocks can also be made into a tea to treat abdominal pain.

Cottonwood:
    Mixing flower buds from cottonwood (available in spring) with fat can be used as a salve that can treat skin infections and treat aching muscles. Sticky resins from the flower buds can also be ingested to treat coughs and pain.

Dandelion:
    The roots of a dandelion can be eaten raw or boiled and ingested to reduce inflammation.

Great Mullein:
    Tea made from mullein flowers can treat pain and act as a sedative. Tea made from mullein stalks can be used to treat cramping. Tea made from mullein leaves have been used as an anti-inflammatory due to its high levels of mucilage. However, tea MUST be strained multiple times to protect throat against tiny fibers on leaves as they can cause irritation.

Juniper:
    Juniper berry tea has been used to reduce swelling and inflammation

Lambs Quarters:
    The leaves of lambs quarters can be used as poultices to treat inflamed eyes.

Maple:
    A tea made from maple tree branches can be applied externally and internally to reduce swelling.

Oak:
    Oak bark can be chewed to relieve toothache pain.

Plantain:

    Ingesting raw leaves and seed stalks of plantains can treat inflammation. The leaves can treat a variety of other issues including sprained and strained muscles, swollen joints and sore feet by heating leaves and applying them to the effected area.

Rabbitbrush:

    Rabbitbrush roots can be boiled into a tea to treat menstrual cramps. Leaves from rabbitbrushes can be applied to decaying teeth to relieve toothache.

Rose:

    Rose leaves can be boiled into a tea to treat heartburn and headaches. The leaves can also be made into a salve to treat mouth sores. When mixed with wine, ground rose leaves can alleviate earaches, uterine cramping and toothaches. Rose seeds can be cooked and eaten to relieve sore muscles.

Sage:

    Sage leaves, soaked in water, can be applied as a poultice to treat infection and swelling.

Salsify:

    Ingesting salsify plants (refer to plant description for edibleness) has been used to relieve heartburn.

Sunflower:

    The flowers of a sunflower can be made into a tea to treat swelling.

Willow:

    The inner bark of the willow tree can be chewed or made into a tea to relieve pain. Willow has many similar chemical properties found in aspirin. Those who are allergic to aspirin should avoid taking willow.

Skin

Burdock:
Burdock leaves have been applied to the skin as a poultice to heal burns, sores, and ulcers. Burdock leaves can also be made into a wash (tea) that can treat hair loss, skin infections, hives, psoriasis and eczema.

Cattail:
Root-stocks can be made into a paste to treat wounds, burns, boils, sores scalds and inflammation.

Clover:
Clover plants can be boiled in water to create a tea to be taken externally to treat skin diseases. Tea made from red clover flowers can be applied externally to treat skin issues such as sores, burns, ulcers, burns and athletes foot.

Cottonwood:
Mixing flower buds from cottonwood (available in spring) with fat can be used as a salve that can treat skin infections. Leaves can be applied to sores, boils, aching muscles and bruises that have been infected by maggots.

Curly Dock:
Dock leaves can be rubbed on the skin to aid rashes caused by stinging nettle. Ingesting the leaves and seeds of dock plants have also been suggested to treat warts and skin sores.

Dandelion:
The milky sap from the dandelion root can be applied three times daily for 7-15 days in order to kill warts.

Great Mullein:
Mullein flowers can be soaked in oil and be used topically to treat warts. Mullein leaves and flowers can be used as a poultice to treat ulcers, hemorrhoids and tumors.

Juniper:
Juniper needles can be dried and made into a powder and applied to skin diseases.

Lambs Quarters:
The leaves of lambs quarters can be used as poultices to treat wounds, swelling and burns.

Oak:

Oak bark tea can be used to treat burns, rashes, cuts and scrapes.

Plantain:

The juices of plantain leaves can be applied to the skin to treat sunburns, sore nipples, poison-ivy rashes, cuts, burns and blisters. A strong tea made out of plantain leaves is said to treat dandruff.

Sage:

Sage leaves, when soaked in water, can be applied as a poultice to treat skin infections, cuts, scrapes and other skin issues.

Smooth Sumac:

The bark from the roots of smooth sumac can be used as a poultice to heal open wounds and ulcers. Leaves that are bruised and moistened can be applied to a variety of rashes, including ones caused by plant irritants such as poison oak, stinging nettles or poison-ivy.

Spruce:

Sap from spruce trees can be mixed with fat to create a salve for treating cuts, rashes, scrapes and burns.

Sunflower:

The flowers and leaves of a sunflower can be made into a poultice and/or a tea to treat blisters.

Thistle:

The leaves of the thistle plant can be made into a medicinal tea to apply externally & internally to treat ulcers, leprosy sores, pimples and rashes.

Willow:

Poultices made from the inner bark can be applied to insect bites, cuts, rashes, cancers, minor burns and scrapes.

Stomach Issues

Cattail:
Flower buds ban be eaten to relieve diarrhea. Root-stocks from the cattail can be made into a tea to treat diarrhea and dysentery.

Dandelion:
The roots of a dandelion can be eaten raw, boiled or made into a tea to act as a laxative.

Oak:
Oak root bark can be boiled to create a tea to regulate bowel problems and to treat diarrhea.

Plantain:
Plantain seeds and seed stalks can be used to make a tea to treat diarrhea due to containing high levels of mucilage.

Rabbitbrush:
Rabbitbrush leaves can be boiled into a tea to treat constipation and other stomach problems.

Rose:
Rose roots can be boiled into a tea and ingested to treat diarrhea and upset stomach.

Sage:
Tea made from sage leaves can treat diarrhea, stomach aches and vomiting.

Salsify:
Ingesting the white sap of salsify plants has been used to cure indigestion.

Smooth Sumac:
The bark of the smooth sumac tree can be made into a tea to treat diarrhea and dysentery.

Spruce:
Tea made from the inner bark of spruce trees can be used to treat stomach problems.

Thistle:
The roots of the thistle plant can be made into a medicinal tea and ingested to relieve dysentery and

diarrhea.

Willow:

Willow bark may be chewed or made into a tea to treat digestive problems and diarrhea.

Urine / Bladder Issues

Aspen:
Tea made from aspen bark has been used to treat urinary tract infections.

Cattail:
Ingesting or chewing root-stocks can be used to increase urination.

Dandelion:
The roots of a dandelion can be made into a tea to stimulate urination and treat urinary tract issues.

Great Mullein:
Tea made from mullein roots can stimulate urination and be used as an overall medicine to improve the bladder. However, tea MUST be strained multiple times to protect throat against tiny fibers on leaves as they can cause irritation.

Juniper:
Juniper berries can be eaten raw to stimulate urination. Juniper berry tea can be used to cleanse kidneys.

Salsify:
Ingesting salsify plants (refer to plant description for edibleness) has been used to stimulate urination.

Smooth Sumac:
Tea made from the root bark can treat painful urination and assist with fluid retention in the body.

www.ingramcontent.com/pod-product-compliance
Lightning Source LLC
Chambersburg PA
CBHW060805270326
41927CB00002B/57